BONIFACE DAAWIEH-KEELSON

THE
GAINS
OF THE
JUST

&

THE
END
OF THE
WICKED

THE GAINS OF
THE JUST
&
THE END OF
THE WICKED

BONIFACE DAAWIEH-KEELSON

THE GAINS OF
THE JUST
&
THE END OF
THE WICKED

COPYRIGHT © BONIFACE & EVELYN KEELSON 2016
PUBLISHED 2016 BY
DAAWIEHBOOKS AND DREAMHAUZ PUBLICATIONS

Published for Worldwide Distribution by:
QUEST PUBLICATIONS
6-176 Henry Street
Brantford, Ontario, N3S 5C8
Canada
Email: questpublications@outlook.com
Website: www.questpub.questforgod.org

Cover Design & Interior Layout / Formatting by:
QUEST PUBLICATIONS

ISBN-13: 978-1-988439-04-4

To share your testimonies with me please write to me on this
address:
Boniface Daawieh-Keelson
DarwiehBooks and Publications
P.O. Box AF 657, Adenta-Accra,
Ghana, West Africa

OR Contact me on the following Cell Phones
001-233 244765586
001-233 244684802

My other contacts are Email:
amawaa@yahoo.com
evangelistboniface@ymail.com
bonifacekeelson@gmail.com

Social Media:
www.facebook.com/boniface.keelson
www.facebook.com/boniface.keelson

All scripture quotations are from the King James Version of
the Bible unless otherwise stated.

Contents

DEDICATION

I dedicate this work to my wife...

Mrs Evelyn Daawieh Keelson

Studying the Bible with you has
always been a blessing.

INTRODUCTION

Recently my wife and I picked up the Book of Job for our devotional study.

TWO great lessons came out clearly in this devotional study.

The lessons are:

I.   THE GAINS OF THE JUST
II. THE END OF THE WICKED

These lessons are what I wish to share with you in this small book.

PART ONE

THE GAINS OF THE JUST
A. CHARACTERISTICS

Firstly, we must establish *who the JUST is*. From the readings of the Book of Job we come to the knowledge that **the JUST is:**

1. **Someone who walks Upright before GOD—Job 1:1, 8**

   There was a man in the land of Uz, whose name was Job; and that man was perfect and upright, and one that feared God, and eschewed evil. And the LORD said unto Satan, Hast thou considered my servant Job, that there is none like him in the earth, a perfect and an upright man, one that feareth God, and escheweth evil?
   (Job 1:1, 8 KJV)

2. Someone who has the Fear of God in his life—Job 1:1, 8

There was a man in the land of Uz, whose name was Job; and that man was perfect and upright, and one that feared God, and eschewed evil. And the LORD said unto Satan, Hast thou considered my servant Job, that there is none like him in the earth, a perfect and an upright man, one that feareth God, and escheweth evil? (Job 1:1, 8 KJV)

3. Someone who Eschews Evil—Job 1:1, 8

There was a man in the land of Uz, whose name was Job; and that man was perfect and upright, and one that feared God, and eschewed evil. And the LORD said unto Satan, Hast thou considered my servant Job, that there is none like him in the earth, a perfect and an upright man, one that feareth God, and escheweth evil? (Job 1:1, 8 KJV)

4. Someone who prays to God AND LOOKS UP to God (has a praying lifestyle)—Job 1:5

And it was so, when the days of their feasting were gone about, that Job sent and sanctified

them, and rose up early in the morning,
and offered burnt offerings according to the
number of them all: for Job said, It may be
that my sons have sinned, and cursed God in
their hearts. Thus did Job continually.
(Job 1:5 KJV)

5. Someone who Accepts Godly rebuke and Godly correction—Job 5:17

Behold, happy is the man whom God
correcteth: therefore despise not thou the
chastening of the Almighty:
(Job 5:17 KJV)

6. Someone who SEEKS after God sincerely—Job 8:5

If thou wouldest seek unto God betimes, and
make thy supplication to the Almighty;
(Job 8:5 KJV)

7. Someone who has a Pure Heart—Job 8:6

If thou wert pure and upright; surely now
he would awake for thee, and make the
habitation of thy righteousness prosperous.
(Job 8:6 KJV)

8. Someone who has Prepared his Heart before God—Job 11:13

If thou prepare thine heart, and stretch out thine hands toward him;
(Job 11:13 KJV)

9. Someone who Agrees with God—Job 22:21

Acquaint now thyself with him, and be at peace: thereby good shall come unto thee.
(Job 22:21 KJV)

10. Someone who Receives the law of God into his heart—Job 22:22

Receive, I pray thee, the law from his mouth, and lay up his words in thine heart.
(Job 22:22 KJV)

11. Someone who Always return to God—Job 22:23

If thou return to the Almighty, thou shalt be built up...
(Job 22:23 KJV)

12. Someone who puts away iniquity from his tabernacle—Job 22:23

...Thou shalt put away iniquity far from thy tabernacles.
(Job 22:23 KJV)

13. Someone who Has a delight in the Almighty God—Job 22:26

For then shalt thou have thy delight in the Almighty, and shalt lift up thy face unto God.
(Job 22:26 KJV)

14. Someone who is Prompt in paying his vows (to God)—Job 22:27

Thou shalt make thy prayer unto him, and he shall hear thee, and thou shalt pay thy vows.
(Job 22:27 KJV)

15. Someone who walks in the spirit of humility. —Job 22:29

When men are cast down, then thou shalt say, There is lifting up; and he shall save the humble person.
(Job 22:29 KJV)

16. Someone with Pure Hands—Job 22:30

He shall deliver the island of the innocent:
and it is delivered by the pureness of thine
hands.
(Job 22:30 KJV)

17. Someone who Walks in the spirit of innocence—Job 22:30

He shall deliver the island of the innocent:
and it is delivered by the pureness of thine
hands.
(Job 22:30 KJV)

18. Someone who follow after the foot steps of God—Job 23:11

My foot hath held his steps...
(Job 23:11 KJV)

19. Someone who never depart from the ways of God—Job 23:11

...His way have I kept, and not declined.
(Job 23:11 KJV)

20. Someone who never goes back from the commandments of God's lips—Job 23:12

Neither have I gone back from the
commandment of his lips...
(Job 23:12 KJV)

21. Someone who values God's word and teachings so highly—Job 23:12

...I have esteemed the words of his mouth
more than my necessary food.
(Job 23:12 KJV)

22. Someone who has a strong fear and reverence for God more than anything else in this world—Job 23:15-17

Therefore am I troubled at his presence:
when I consider, I am afraid of him. For God
maketh my heart soft, and the Almighty
troubleth me: Because I was not cut off before
the darkness, neither hath he covered the
darkness from my face.
(Job 23:15-17 KJV)

23. Someone who avoids all forms of immoral lifestyle—Job 31:1

I made a covenant with mine eyes; why then should I think upon a maid?
(Job 31:1 KJV)

24. Someone who is always conscious of the judgement of God—Job 31:5-6

If I have walked with vanity, or if my foot hath hasted to deceit; Let me be weighed in an even balance, that God may know mine integrity.
(Job 31:5-6 KJV)

25. Someone who values other humans highly, irrespective of their status or background—Job 31:13-15

If I did despise the cause of my manservant or of my maidservant, when they contended with me; What then shall I do when God riseth up? and when he visiteth, what shall I answer him? Did not he that made me in the womb make him? and did not one fashion us in the womb?
(Job 31:13-15 KJV)

26. Someone who does not consider money to be everything in life—Job 31:24-25

If I have made gold my hope, or have said to the fine gold, Thou art my confidence; If I rejoiced because my wealth was great, and because mine hand had gotten much; (Job 31:24-25 KJV)

27. Someone who is absolutely loyal to God— Job 31:26-28

If I beheld the sun when it shined, or the moon walking in brightness; And my heart hath been secretly enticed, or my mouth hath kissed my hand: This also were an iniquity to be punished by the judge: for I should have denied the God that is above. (Job 31:26-28 KJV)

28. Someone who does not cover his transgressions and pretend to be Godly— Job 31:33

If I covered my transgressions as Adam, by hiding mine iniquity in my bosom: (Job 31:33 KJV)

29. Some who delights in obeying God—Job 36:11

If they obey and serve him, they shall spend their days in prosperity, and their years in pleasures.
(Job 36:11 KJV)

30. Someone who willingly serves God Almighty—Job 36:11

If they obey and serve him, they shall spend their days in prosperity, and their years in pleasures.
(Job 36:11 KJV)

B. THE GAINS

According to the Book of JOB, here are some of *the gains of the just person* described heretofore:

1. He Enjoys a Great Family—Job 1:2

And there were born unto him seven sons and three daughters.
(Job 1:2 KJV)

2. He Gets Blessed with Great Substance in life—Job 1:3

His substance also was seven thousand sheep, and three thousand camels, and five hundred yoke of oxen, and five hundred she asses, and a very great household; so that this man was the greatest of all the men of the east.
(Job 1:3 KJV)

3. He Enjoys the strong hedge of God's protection—Job 1:10

Hast not thou made an hedge about him, and about his house, and about all that he hath on every side? thou hast blessed the work of his hands, and his substance is increased in the

land.
(Job 1:10 KJV)

4. He Enjoys deliverance from all forms of troubles—Job 5:19

He shall deliver thee in six troubles: yea, in seven there shall no evil touch thee.
(Job 5:19 KJV)

5. God hides him from the scourge of the tongue—Job 5:21

Thou shalt be hid from the scourge of the tongue: neither shalt thou be afraid of destruction when it cometh.
(Job 5:21 KJV)

6. God delivers him from common destruction and disaster—Job 5:21-22

Thou shalt be hid from the scourge of the tongue: neither shalt thou be afraid of destruction when it cometh. At destruction and famine thou shalt laugh: neither shalt thou be afraid of the beasts of the earth.
(Job 5:21-22 KJV)

7. **Even nature and natural forces rises up to his aid in life—Job 5:23**

For thou shalt be in league with the stones of the field: and the beasts of the field shall be at peace with thee.
(Job 5:23 KJV)

8. **He Enjoys the visitations of God—Job 5:24**

And thou shalt know that thy tabernacle shall be in peace; and thou shalt visit thy habitation, and shalt not sin.
(Job 5:24 KJV)

9. **His children shall be great in life—Job 5:25**

Thou shalt know also that thy seed shall be great, and thine offspring as the grass of the earth.
(Job 5:25 KJV)

10. **He shall come to old age...He shall not be cut off in the midst of his years—Job 5:26**

Thou shalt come to thy grave in a full age, like as a shock of corn cometh in in his season.
(Job 5:26 KJV)

11. God Himself would awake for him—Job 8:6

If thou wert pure and upright; surely now he would awake for thee, and make the habitation of thy righteousness prosperous.
(Job 8:6 KJV)

12. God would let him experience an all round prosperity in life—Job 8:6

If thou wert pure and upright; surely now he would awake for thee, and make the habitation of thy righteousness prosperous.
(Job 8:6 KJV)

13. He shall surely experience the increase of God—Job 8:7

Though thy beginning was small, yet thy latter end should greatly increase.
(Job 8:7 KJV)

14. God would fill his mouth (full) with laughter—Job 8:21

Till he fill thy mouth with laughing, and thy lips with rejoicing.
(Job 8:21 KJV)

15. God would personally shame all his enemies—Job 8:22

They that hate thee shall be clothed with shame; and the dwelling place of the wicked shall come to nought.
(Job 8:22 KJV)

16. He would certainly enjoy the favour of God—Job 10:12

Thou hast granted me life and favour...
(Job 10:12 KJV)

17. God Himself preserves him—Job 10:12

...Thy visitation hath preserved my spirit.
(Job 10:12 KJV)

18. He shall always have confidence in the presence of God—Job 11:15

For then shalt thou lift up thy face without spot; yea, thou shalt be stedfast, and shalt not fear:
(Job 11:15 KJV)

19. He shall be Healthy (enjoy good health) even in old age—Job 11:17

And thine age shall be clearer than the noonday; thou shalt shine forth, thou shalt be

as the morning.
(Job 11:17 KJV)

20. He would no doubt shine in this life—Job 11:17

...thou shalt shine forth, thou shalt be as the morning.
(Job 11:17 KJV)

21. God shall grant him divine security and safety—Job 11:18-19

And thou shalt be secure, because there is hope; yea, thou shalt dig about thee, and thou shalt take thy rest in safety.
(Job 11:18 KJV)

22. He shall grow stronger and stronger always—Job 17:9

The righteous also shall hold on his way, and he that hath clean hands shall be stronger and stronger.
(Job 17:9 KJV)

23. He will always be at peace in life—Job 22:21, Job 5:24

Acquaint now thyself with him, and be at peace: thereby good shall come unto thee.
(Job 22:21 KJV)

And thou shalt know that thy tabernacle
shall be in peace; and thou shalt visit thy
habitation, and shalt not sin.
(Job 5:24 KJV)

24. God would continue to build him up in life—Job 22:23

If thou return to the Almighty, thou shalt be
built up, thou shalt put away iniquity far from
thy tabernacles.
(Job 22:23 KJV)

25. He would in no doubt enjoy financial prosperity—Job 22:24-25

Then shalt thou lay up gold as dust, and the
gold of Ophir as the stones of the brooks. Yea,
the Almighty shall be thy defence, and thou
shalt have plenty of silver.
(Job 22:24-25 KJV)

26. God Himself shall forever become his defense—Job 22:25

Yea, the Almighty shall be thy defence, and
thou shalt have plenty of silver.
(Job 22:25 KJV)

27. His prayers are quickly answered—Job 22:27

Thou shalt make thy prayer unto him, and he shall hear thee, and thou shalt pay thy vows.
(Job 22:27 KJV)

28. All his wish becomes established—Job 22:28

Thou shalt also decree a thing, and it shall be established unto thee...
(Job 22:28 KJV)

29. He would keep shining and shining in life—Job 22:28

...the light shall shine upon thy ways.
(Job 22:28 KJV)

30. He would be restored in all areas from the Lord—Job 22:29

When men are cast down, then thou shalt say, There is lifting up; and he shall save the humble person.
(Job 22:29 KJV)

31. He would always enjoy the lifting of God—Job 22:29

When men are cast down, then thou shalt say, There is lifting up; and he shall save the humble person.
(Job 22:29 KJV)

32. God shall continue to rescue him because of his innocency—Job 22:30

He shall deliver the island of the innocent: and it is delivered by the pureness of thine hands.
(Job 22:30 KJV)

33. GOD would never withdraw His eyes from him (for good)—Job 36:7

He withdraweth not his eyes from the righteous: but with kings are they on the throne; yea, he doth establish them for ever, and they are exalted.
(Job 36:7 KJV)

34. God Himself would ensure his enthronement...make him rule in life like a king—Job 36:7

He withdraweth not his eyes from the righteous: but with kings are they on the

throne; yea, he doth establish them for ever,
and they are exalted.
(Job 36:7 KJV)

35. God would surely establish and honour him always—Job 36:7

He withdraweth not his eyes from the righteous: but with kings are they on the throne; yea, he doth establish them for ever, and they are exalted.
(Job 36:7 KJV)

36. He is bound to enjoy the benevolence of God and the good pleasures of life—Job 36:11

If they obey and serve him, they shall spend their days in prosperity, and their years in pleasures.
(Job 36:11 KJV)

37. God shall continue to exalt him always—Job 36:7

He withdraweth not his eyes from the righteous: but with kings are they on the throne; yea, he doth establish them for ever, and they are exalted.
(Job 36:7 KJV)

38. God would turn all his calamities into testimonies—Job 42:10

And the LORD turned the captivity of Job, when he prayed for his friends: also the LORD gave Job twice as much as he had before.
(Job 42:10 KJV)

39. God shall gives him double for all his troubles—Job 42:10

...the LORD gave Job twice as much as he had before.
(Job 42:10 KJV)

40. God shall bless him with a glorious end— Job 42:10-17

And the LORD turned the captivity of Job, when he prayed for his friends: also the LORD gave Job twice as much as he had before. Then came there unto him all his brethren, and all his sisters, and all they that had been of his acquaintance before, and did eat bread with him in his house: and they bemoaned him, and comforted him over all the evil that the LORD had brought upon him: every man also gave him a piece of money, and every one an earring of gold. So the LORD blessed the latter end of Job

more than his beginning: for he had fourteen
thousand sheep, and six thousand camels,
and a thousand yoke of oxen, and a thousand
she asses. He had also seven sons and three
daughters. And he called the name of the first,
Jemima; and the name of the second, Kezia;
and the name of the third, Kerenhappuch.
And in all the land were no women found so
fair as the daughters of Job: and their father
gave them inheritance among their brethren.
After this lived Job an hundred and forty
years, and saw his sons, and his sons' sons,
even four generations. So Job died, being old
and full of days.
(Job 42:10-17 KJV)

C. EXCEPTIONS

Ceteris Paribus is a common latin phrase. The common English idiom ALL THINGS BEING EQUAL is the direct translation of the Latin phrase *ceteris paribus*. Among the number of meanings of this common idiom is that; if everything happen as expected. This is because sometimes there could be a set out expectation for a certain result based on certain inputs but the results turn out differently. In the same vein the book of Job outlines a number of gains a just man is bound to experience in this life but in reality sometimes one might come across a case of a just man (like the bitter experience of Job) which is an exception. For example; one might come across a just man who is challenged with:

1. An unhappy life—Job 21:25

And another dieth in the bitterness of his soul, and never eateth with pleasure.
(Job 21:25 KJV)

2. Having bitter experiences—Job 21:25

And another dieth in the bitterness of his soul,
and never eateth with pleasure.
(Job 21:25 KJV)

3. Having helped others before who now treat him so bad—job 30:1-8

But now they that are younger than I have
me in derision, whose fathers I would have
disdained to have set with the dogs of my
flock. Yea, whereto might the strength of
their hands profit me, in whom old age was
perished? For want and famine they were
solitary; fleeing into the wilderness in former
time desolate and waste. Who cut up mallows
by the bushes, and juniper roots for their
meat. They were driven forth from among
men, (they cried after them as after a thief;)
To dwell in the clifts of the valleys, in caves of
the earth, and in the rocks. Among the bushes
they brayed; under the nettles they were
gathered together. They were children of fools,
yea, children of base men: they were viler than
the earth.
(Job 30:1-8 KJV)

4. **Waiting on the Lord for good but instead evil shows up—Job 30:26**

   When I looked for good, then evil came unto me: and when I waited for light, there came darkness.
   (Job 30:26 KJV)

5. **Expecting light to shine for him but gloom arrives—Job 30:26**

   When I looked for good, then evil came unto me: and when I waited for light, there came darkness.
   (Job 30:26 KJV)

6. **Confronted with all forms and shapes of afflictions—Job 30:27**

   My bowels boiled, and rested not: the days of affliction prevented me.
   (Job 30:27 KJV)

7. **Experiencing so much emotional pain and weeping—Job 30:31**

   My harp also is turned to mourning, and my organ into the voice of them that weep.
   (Job 30:31 KJV)

We may not be able to explain fully why these exceptions might be the case in the lives of certain just persons. However the Book of Job points out two clear reasons why things could be so:

1. **There could be bitter lessons God is allowing one to go through for His own purpose—Job 36:15**

   He delivereth the poor in his affliction, and openeth their ears in oppression.
   (Job 36:15 KJV)

2. **There could be experiences God allows one to go through in order to appreciate the good side of life when they fully come—Job 36:16**

   Even so would he have removed thee out of the strait into a broad place, where there is no straitness; and that which should be set on thy table should be full of fatness.
   (Job 36:16 KJV)

PART TWO

THE END OF THE WICKED

A. CHARACTERISTICS

It is important to establish in this section **who the WICKED is**. From the study of the Book of Job we come to the knowledge that **the WICKED is:**

1. **Someone who walks in craftiness—Job 5:12**

    He disappointeth the devices of the crafty, so that their hands cannot perform their enterprise.
    (Job 5:12 KJV)

2. **Someone who is wiser in his own eyes and ways (more than the counsel of God)—Job 5:13**

    He taketh the wise in their own craftiness: and the counsel of the froward is carried headlong. (Job 5:13 KJV)

3. **Someone who practices frowardness—Job 5:13**

    He taketh the wise in their own craftiness: and the counsel of the froward is carried headlong. (Job 5:13 KJV)

4. **Someone who takes advantage of orphans and helpless people—Job 6:27**

    Yea, ye overwhelm the fatherless... (Job 6:27 KJV)

5. **SOMEONE who betrays and digs a pit for a friend—Job 6:27**

    ...ye dig a pit for your friend. (Job 6:27 KJV)

6. **Someone who forgets God—Job 8:13**

    So are the paths of all that forget God; and the hypocrite's hope shall perish: (Job 8:13 KJV)

7.   Someone who walks in hypocrisy—Job 8:13

So are the paths of all that forget God; and the hypocrite's hope shall perish:
(Job 8:13 KJV)

8.   Someone who is simply an evil doer—Job 8:20

Behold, God will not cast away a perfect man, neither will he help the evil doers:
(Job 8:20 KJV)

9.   Someone who hardens himself on and before God—Job 9:4

He is wise in heart, and mighty in strength: who hath hardened himself against him, and hath prospered?
(Job 9:4 KJV)

10.   Someone who has become vain in his thoughts and ways—Job 11:11

For he knoweth vain men: he seeth wickedness also; will he not then consider it?
(Job 11:11 KJV)

11. Someone who practices robbery and robs for a living—Job 12:6

The tabernacles of robbers prosper, and they that provoke God are secure; into whose hand God bringeth abundantly.
(Job 12:6 KJV)

12. Someone who lives his lifestyle just to provoke God and Christian virtues—Job 12:6

The tabernacles of robbers prosper, and they that provoke God are secure; into whose hand God bringeth abundantly.
(Job 12:6 KJV)

13. Someone who forges lies—Job 13:4

But ye are forgers of lies, ye are all physicians of no value.
(Job 13:4 KJV)

14. Someone who turns against God—Job 15:13

That thou turnest thy spirit against God, and lettest such words go out of thy mouth?
(Job 15:13 KJV)

15. Someone who stretches his hand against God (against the church)—Job 15:25

For he stretcheth out his hand against
God, and strengtheneth himself against the
Almighty.
(Job 15:25 KJV)

16. Someone who makes bribery a way of life—Job 15:34

For the congregation of hypocrites shall
be desolate, and fire shall consume the
tabernacles of bribery.
(Job 15:34 KJV)

17. Someone who conceives mischief—Job 15:35

They conceive mischief, and bring forth
vanity, and their belly prepareth deceit.
(Job 15:35 KJV)

18. Someone whose bones are full of sins—Job 20:11

His bones are full of the sin of his youth,
which shall lie down with him in the dust.
(Job 20:11 KJV)

19. Someone who delights in playing wicked—Job 20:12

Though wickedness be sweet in his mouth,
though he hide it under his tongue;
(Job 20:12 KJV)

20. Someone who forcefully swallows up what belongs to others—Job 20:15-16

He hath swallowed down riches, and he shall
vomit them up again: God shall cast them out
of his belly. He shall suck the poison of asps:
the viper's tongue shall slay him.
(Job 20:15-16 KJV)

21. Someone who oppress and forsakes the poor—Job 20:19

Because he hath oppressed and hath forsaken
the poor; because he hath violently taken away
an house which he builded not;
(Job 20:19 KJV)

22. Someone who violently takes away the properties of others—Job 20:19

Because he hath oppressed and hath forsaken
the poor; because he hath violently taken away
an house which he builded not;
(Job 20:19 KJV)

23. Someone who has no serious regard for God—Job 21:14

Therefore they say unto God, Depart from us; for we desire not the knowledge of thy ways. (Job 21:14 KJV)

24. Someone who is not so interested in the teachings of God—Job 21:14

Therefore they say unto God, Depart from us; for we desire not the knowledge of thy ways. (Job 21:14 KJV)

25. Someone who does not care much about the will of God concerning his life...Job 21:14

Therefore they say unto God, Depart from us; for we desire not the knowledge of thy ways. (Job 21:14 KJV)

26. Someone who does not see the need to serve God—Job 21:15

What is the Almighty, that we should serve him? and what profit should we have, if we pray unto him? (Job 21:15 KJV)

THE END OF THE WICKED

27. **Someone who cares less about offering his service to God—Job 21:15**

What is the Almighty, that we should serve him? and what profit should we have, if we pray unto him?
(Job 21:15 KJV)

28. **Someone who considers prayer as something not so important—Job 21:15**

What is the Almighty, that we should serve him? and what profit should we have, if we pray unto him?
(Job 21:15 KJV)

29. **Someone who thinks those who spend much time praying and going to church are unwise—Job 21:15**

What is the Almighty, that we should serve him? and what profit should we have, if we pray unto him?
(Job 21:15 KJV)

30. **Someone with the notion that he is self made—Job 21:16**

Lo, their good is not in their hand: the counsel of the wicked is far from me.
(Job 21:16 KJV)

31. Someone who is a schemer and a cheater—Job 24:2

Some remove the landmarks; they violently take away flocks, and feed thereof.
(Job 24:2 KJV)

32. Someone who is heartless towards orphans/widows and the helpless—Job 24:3-11

They drive away the ass of the fatherless, they take the widow's ox for a pledge. They turn the needy out of the way: the poor of the earth hide themselves together. Behold, as wild asses in the desert, go they forth to their work; rising betimes for a prey: the wilderness yieldeth food for them and for their children. They reap every one his corn in the field: and they gather the vintage of the wicked. They cause the naked to lodge without clothing, that they have no covering in the cold. They are wet with the showers of the mountains, and embrace the rock for want of a shelter. They pluck the fatherless from the breast, and take a pledge of the poor. They cause him to go naked without clothing, and they take away the sheaf from the hungry; Which make oil within their walls, and tread their winepresses, and suffer thirst.
(Job 24:3-11 KJV)

33. Someone who rebels against the light.... (operates his enterprise in darkness)—Job 24:13

They are of those that rebel against the light; they know not the ways thereof, nor abide in the paths thereof.
(Job 24:13 KJV)

34. Someone who is a murderer—Job 24:14

The murderer rising with the light killeth the poor and needy, and in the night is as a thief.
(Job 24:14 KJV)

35. Someone who is adulterous and a womanizer—Job 24:15

The eye also of the adulterer waiteth for the twilight, saying, No eye shall see me: and disguiseth his face.
(Job 24:15 KJV)

36. Someone who denies God—Job 31:28

This also were an iniquity to be punished by the judge: for I should have denied the God that is above.
(Job 31:28 KJV)

37. Someone who turns back from God and will not consider any of His ways—Job 34:27

Because they turned back from him, and
would not consider any of his ways:
(Job 34:27 KJV)

38. Someone who is very prideful in life—Job 35:12

There they cry, but none giveth answer,
because of the pride of evil men.
(Job 35:12 KJV)

39. Someone who is simply Godless—Job 36:13

But the hypocrites in heart heap up wrath:
they cry not when he bindeth them.
(Job 36:13 KJV)

40. Someone who pours his anger at God and the church for any mishap in life—Job 36:13

But the hypocrites in heart heap up wrath:
they cry not when he bindeth them.
(Job 36:13 KJV)

B. THE END

From the characteristics of the wicked above, we can conclude that the WICKED is the ungodly, corrupt persons, perpetuaters of evil, haters of Godliness, vain persons, hypocrites, and persons without the fear of God.

The book of Job establishes a number of mishaps that are likely to befall *such Wicked persons.*

1. **The habitation of the wicked is more often under a curse—Job 5:3**

   I have seen the foolish taking root: but suddenly I cursed his habitation.
   (Job 5:3 KJV)

2. **The children of the wicked are far from safety—Job 5:4**

   His children are far from safety, and they are crushed in the gate, neither is there any to deliver them.
   (Job 5:4 KJV)

3. Strange attacks of wicked magnitude may visit the wicked—Job 5:5

Whose harvest the hungry eateth up, and taketh it even out of the thorns, and the robber swalloweth up their substance.
(Job 5:5 KJV)

4. The wicked are bound to suffer numerous afflictions and troubles—Job 5:6-7

Although affliction cometh not forth of the dust, neither doth trouble spring out of the ground; Yet man is born unto trouble, as the sparks fly upward.
(Job 5:6-7 KJV)

5. Darkness shall visit the wicked in broad day light—Job 5:14

They meet with darkness in the daytime, and grope in the noonday as in the night.
(Job 5:14 KJV)

6. Confusion shall become the portion of the wicked—Job 5:14

They meet with darkness in the daytime, and grope in the noonday as in the night.
(Job 5:14 KJV)

7. **The wicked shall surely end up as nothing—Job 6:18**

    The paths of their way are turned aside; they go to nothing, and perish.
    (Job 6:18 KJV)

8. **The wicked shall be scared with terrible dreams and visions—Job 7:14**

    Then thou scarest me with dreams, and terrifiest me through visions:
    (Job 7:14 KJV)

9. **All the hopes of the wicked shall perish—Job 8:13**

    So are the paths of all that forget God; and the hypocrite's hope shall perish:
    (Job 8:13 KJV)

10. **God will certainly cut off the wicked—Job 11:10**

    If he cut off, and shut up, or gather together, then who can hinder him?
    (Job 11:10 KJV)

11. The Almighty will cause the wicked to be shut off at the right time—Job 11:10

If he cut off, and shut up, or gather together, then who can hinder him?
(Job 11:10 KJV)

12. The eyes of the wicked shall be caused to fail—Job 11:20

But the eyes of the wicked shall fail, and they shall not escape, and their hope shall be as the giving up of the ghost.
(Job 11:20 KJV)

13. The wicked shall never escape forever—Job 11:20

But the eyes of the wicked shall fail, and they shall not escape, and their hope shall be as the giving up of the ghost.
(Job 11:20 KJV)

14. The LIFE of the wicked shall no doubt spoil—Job 12:17

He leadeth counsellors away spoiled, and maketh the judges fools.
(Job 12:17 KJV)

15. The Almighty shall cause the wicked to make a fool out of his life—Job 12:17

He leadeth counsellors away spoiled, and maketh the judges fools.
(Job 12:17 KJV)

16. The wicked shall definitely be overthrown at the set time—Job 12:19

He leadeth princes away spoiled, and overthroweth the mighty.
(Job 12:19 KJV)

17. God will one day break all the defenses of the wicked—Job 12:20

He removeth away the speech of the trusty, and taketh away the understanding of the aged.
(Job 12:20 KJV)

18. God has what it takes to make the wicked contemptible—Job 12:21

He poureth contempt upon princes, and weakeneth the strength of the mighty.
(Job 12:21 KJV)

19. God can make the wicked groove in perpetual darkness—Job 12:24-25

He taketh away the heart of the chief of the people of the earth, and causeth them to wander in a wilderness where there is no way. They grope in the dark without light, and he maketh them to stagger like a drunken man. (Job 12:24-25 KJV)

20. They shall be made to stagger in broad day light—Job 12:24-25

He taketh away the heart of the chief of the people of the earth, and causeth them to wander in a wilderness where there is no way. They grope in the dark without light, and he maketh them to stagger like a drunken man. (Job 12:24-25 KJV)

21. Unbearable issues of life may visit the wicked and completely wear him out—Job 14:19

The waters wear the stones: thou washest away the things which grow out of the dust of the earth; and thou destroyest the hope of man. (Job 14:19 KJV)

22. The Almighty might strike the wicked and totally change his Countenance and make him distasteable—Job 14:20

Thou prevailest for ever against him, and he passeth: thou changest his countenance, and sendest him away.
(Job 14:20 KJV)

23. The flesh of the wicked might never escape strange infliction of pain—Job 14:21-22, Job 15:20

His sons come to honour, and he knoweth it not; and they are brought low, but he perceiveth it not of them. But his flesh upon him shall have pain, and his soul within him shall mourn.
(Job 14:21-22 KJV)

The wicked man travaileth with pain all his days, and the number of years is hidden to the oppressor.
(Job 15:20 KJV)

24. The soul of the wicked would surely be visited by unbearable sorrow and anguish—Job 14:21-22, Job 15:20

His sons come to honour, and he knoweth it not; and they are brought low, but he

perceiveth it not of them. But his flesh upon him shall have pain, and his soul within him shall mourn.
(Job 14:21-22 KJV)

The wicked man travaileth with pain all his days, and the number of years is hidden to the oppressor.
(Job 15:20 KJV)

25. The wicked shall be terrified at the end of his wickedness with a horrifying sound— Job 15:21

A dreadful sound is in his ears: in prosperity the destroyer shall come upon him.
(Job 15:21 KJV)

26. God Himself shall ensure that the wicked is visited with trouble and anguish in this life—Job 15:24

Trouble and anguish shall make him afraid; they shall prevail against him, as a king ready to the battle.
(Job 15:24 KJV)

27. The Lord shall in no doubt dry up the branches of the wicked in due time—Job 15:30

He shall not depart out of darkness; the flame shall dry up his branches, and by the breath of his mouth shall he go away.
(Job 15:30 KJV)

28. The wicked shall be visited with uncommon leanness and wrinkles in the midst of his years—Job 16:8

And thou hast filled me with wrinkles, which is a witness against me: and my leanness rising up in me beareth witness to my face.
(Job 16:8 KJV)

29. The Lord shall one day deliver the wicked into the hands of his enemies—Job 16:11

God hath delivered me to the ungodly, and turned me over into the hands of the wicked.
(Job 16:11 KJV)

30. Surely the wicked shall end up in life as a byword and a proverb—Job 17:6

He hath made me also a byword of the people; and aforetime I was as a tabret.
(Job 17:6 KJV)

31. The lights of the wicked shall be put off... the wicked would not always shine—Job 18:5

Yea, the light of the wicked shall be put out, and the spark of his fire shall not shine.
(Job 18:5 KJV)

32. Wickedness shall surely take out the shine of the wicked—Job 18:5-6

Yea, the light of the wicked shall be put out, and the spark of his fire shall not shine. The light shall be dark in his tabernacle, and his candle shall be put out with him.
(Job 18:5-6 KJV)

33. Darkness and gloominess shall definitely visit the wicked in this life—Job 18:6

The light shall be dark in his tabernacle, and his candle shall be put out with him.
(Job 18:6 KJV)

34. The wicked is bound to fall into a trap and a snare in this life—Job 18:10

The snare is laid for him in the ground, and a trap for him in the way.
(Job 18:10 KJV)

35. Terrors and Nightmares shall forever become the portion of the wicked—Job 18:11

Terrors shall make him afraid on every side, and shall drive him to his feet.
(Job 18:11 KJV)

36. The physical strength and energy of the wicked shall not be spared in the day God begins to deal with him—Job 18:12

His strength shall be hungerbitten, and destruction shall be ready at his side.
(Job 18:12 KJV)

37. Destruction and emptiness both awaits the wicked at a very significant junction of his life—Job 18:12

His strength shall be hungerbitten, and destruction shall be ready at his side.
(Job 18:12 KJV)

38. Indeed, the very roots of the wicked shall dry up and wither in the day Jehovah shall strike on him—Job 18:16

His roots shall be dried up beneath, and above shall his branch be cut off.
(Job 18:16 KJV)

39. The ways and the top connections of the wicked shall soon be blocked—Job 19:8

He hath fenced up my way that I cannot pass, and he hath set darkness in my paths.
(Job 19:8 KJV)

40. Instead of light, the Lord Himself shall set darkness on the path of the wicked—Job 19:8

He hath fenced up my way that I cannot pass, and he hath set darkness in my paths.
(Job 19:8 KJV)

41. In the day the Almighty shall strike, the wicked shall be striped of all his honor— Job 19:9

He hath stripped me of my glory, and taken the crown from my head.
(Job 19:9 KJV)

42. In the day the Almighty shall strike, the wicked shall be destroyed on every side— Job 19:10

He hath destroyed me on every side, and I am gone: and mine hope hath he removed like a tree.
(Job 19:10 KJV)

43. No matter how well the wicked flourishes, he shall only triumph for a moment—Job 20:5

That the triumphing of the wicked is short, and the joy of the hypocrite but for a moment?
(Job 20:5 KJV)

44. One great truth is that the wicked would soon perish—Job 20:7

Yet he shall perish for ever like his own dung: they which have seen him shall say, Where is he?
(Job 20:7 KJV)

45. A wicked person might be chased out in the midst of his assignment or enterprise—Job 20:8

He shall fly away as a dream, and shall not be found: yea, he shall be chased away as a vision of the night.
(Job 20:8 KJV)

46. The wicked shall one day be forced to vomit whatever he has forcefully swallowed—Job 20:15

He hath swallowed down riches, and he shall vomit them up again: God shall cast them out of his belly.
(Job 20:15 KJV)

47. Some of the things the wicked has forcefully swallowed would turn into poison in his system and kill him—Job 20:16

He shall suck the poison of asps: the viper's tongue shall slay him.
(Job 20:16 KJV)

48. A wicked person might be visited or tortured with strange stomach ailment—Job 20:20

Surely he shall not feel quietness in his belly, he shall not save of that which he desired.
(Job 20:20 KJV)

49. Terrible leanness may visit the wicked— Job 20:21

There shall none of his meat be left; therefore shall no man look for his goods.
(Job 20:21 KJV)

50. The wicked may surely get away with some of their wickedness but certainly not all— Job 20:24

He shall flee from the iron weapon, and the bow of steel shall strike him through.
(Job 20:24 KJV)

51. The wicked shall be visited with terrors upon terrors—Job 20:25

It is drawn, and cometh out of the body; yea, the glittering sword cometh out of his gall: terrors are upon him.
(Job 20:25 KJV)

52. Strange darkness shall surely visit the wicked—Job 20:26

All darkness shall be hid in his secret places: a fire not blown shall consume him; it shall go ill with him that is left in his tabernacle.
(Job 20:26 KJV)

53. Heaven and the Heaven of Heavens will surely expose the wicked—Job 20:27

The heaven shall reveal his iniquity; and the earth shall rise up against him.
(Job 20:27 KJV)

54. The earth and all forces of nature will one day definitely fight the wicked—Job 20:27

The heaven shall reveal his iniquity; and the earth shall rise up against him.
(Job 20:27 KJV)

55. The increase of the house of the wicked shall develop wings and depart—Job 20:28

The increase of his house shall depart, and his goods shall flow away in the day of his wrath.
(Job 20:28 KJV)

56. Snares and sudden fear surely awaits the wicked—Job 22:10

Therefore snares are round about thee, and sudden fear troubleth thee;
(Job 22:10 KJV)

57. The wicked shall one day be swept away like flood—Job 24:18

He is swift as the waters; their portion is cursed in the earth: he beholdeth not the way of the vineyards.
(Job 24:18 KJV)

58. The land (house) the wicked dwells on is under a perpetual curse—Job 24:18

He is swift as the waters; their portion is cursed in the earth: he beholdeth not the way of the vineyards.
(Job 24:18 KJV)

59. The prosperity of the wicked is only for a while—Job 24:23

Though it be given him to be in safety, whereon he resteth; yet his eyes are upon their ways.
(Job 24:23 KJV)

60. God surely keeps an eye on the wicked for destruction—Job 24:23

Though it be given him to be in safety, whereon he resteth; yet his eyes are upon their ways.
(Job 24:23 KJV)

61. There is definitely no hope of eternity for the wicked—Job 27:8

For what is the hope of the hypocrite, though he hath gained, when God taketh away his soul?
(Job 27:8 KJV)

62. In the day when unimaginable trouble and calamity shall visit the wicked his cry shall not be heard—Job 27:9

Will God hear his cry when trouble cometh upon him?
(Job 27:9 KJV)

63. The FUTURE of all wicked persons is already dark and bleak—Job 27:13-18

This is the portion of a wicked man with God, and the heritage of oppressors, which they shall receive of the Almighty. If his children be multiplied, it is for the sword: and his offspring shall not be satisfied with bread. Those that remain of him shall be buried in death: and his widows shall not weep. Though he heap up silver as the dust, and prepare raiment as the clay; He may prepare it, but the just shall put it on, and the innocent shall divide the silver. He buildeth his house as a

moth, and as a booth that the keeper maketh.
(Job 27:13-18 KJV)

64. Terror shall strike the wicked suddenly as he journeys through life—Job 27:20

Terrors take hold on him as waters, a tempest stealeth him away in the night.
(Job 27:20 KJV)

65. The wicked is already given to the wind and storms...A strange wind would definitely visit him in this life—Job 27:21-23

The east wind carrieth him away, and he departeth: and as a storm hurleth him out of his place. For God shall cast upon him, and not spare: he would fain flee out of his hand. Men shall clap their hands at him, and shall hiss him out of his place.
(Job 27:21-23 KJV)

66. Destruction and a strange punishment would never elude the wicked in life—Job 31:3

Is not destruction to the wicked? and a strange punishment to the workers of iniquity?
(Job 31:3 KJV)

67. The wicked may sow and another would reap—Job 31:7-8

If my step hath turned out of the way, and mine heart walked after mine eyes, and if any blot hath cleaved to mine hands; Then let me sow, and let another eat; yea, let my offspring be rooted out.
(Job 31:7-8 KJV)

68. Briers may grow for the wicked when he is looking forward for wheat, and poisonous weeds when he is looking for barley—Job 31:40

Let thistles grow instead of wheat, and cockle instead of barley...
(Job 31:40 KJV)

69. The life of the wicked shall surely be devoid of the preservation by the Almighty—Job 36:6

He preserveth not the life of the wicked: but giveth right to the poor.
(Job 36:6 KJV)

70. Disgrace and unimaginable shame shall decorate the end of the wicked—Job 36:14

They die in youth, and their life is among the unclean.

(Job 36:14 KJV)

C. EXCEPTIONS

Just as there could be exceptional cases of the just or the righteous going through bitter challenges in life—.similarly, there are ***exceptional cases*** pointed out in the book of Job where a wicked person:

1. **May grow very old in life—Job 21:7**

   Wherefore do the wicked live, become old, yea, are mighty in power?
   (Job 21:7 KJV)

2. **May prosper and enjoy good life—Job 21:7**

   Wherefore do the wicked live, become old, yea, are mighty in power?
   (Job 21:7 KJV)

3. **May have such a sweet family—Job 21:8**

   Their seed is established in their sight with them, and their offspring before their eyes.
   (Job 21:8 KJV)

4. **May enjoy peace and live in safety all his life—Job 21:9**

    Their houses are safe from fear, neither is the rod of God upon them.
    (Job 21:9 KJV)

5. **May have a good and a prosperous business—Job 21:10**

    Their bull gendereth, and faileth not; their cow calveth, and casteth not her calf.
    (Job 21:10 KJV)

6. **May live an enjoyable and a joyful life—Job 21:12-13**

    They take the timbrel and harp, and rejoice at the sound of the organ. They spend their days in wealth, and in a moment go down to the grave.
    (Job 21:12-13 KJV)

7. **Whose light might never go off—Job 21:17**

    How oft is the candle of the wicked put out! and how oft cometh their destruction upon them! God distributeth sorrows in his anger.
    (Job 21:17 KJV)

8. **Who may never experience disaster or destruction—Job 21:17**

    How oft is the candle of the wicked put out!
    and how oft cometh their destruction upon
    them! God distributeth sorrows in his anger.
    (Job 21:17 KJV)

9. **Who may never seem to experience the anger and punishment of God—Job 21:17**

    How oft is the candle of the wicked put out!
    and how oft cometh their destruction upon
    them! God distributeth sorrows in his anger.
    (Job 21:17 KJV)

10. **Who may never experience storms and terrible challenges—Job 21:18**

    They are as stubble before the wind, and as
    chaff that the storm carrieth away.
    (Job 21:18 KJV)

11. **Who may stay healthy till the day of his death—Job 21:23-24**

    One dieth in his full strength, being wholly
    at ease and quiet. His breasts are full of milk,
    and his bones are moistened with marrow.
    (Job 21:23-24 KJV)

12. Who is so celebrated both in life and in death—Job 21:23-24, 32-33

One dieth in his full strength, being wholly
at ease and quiet. His breasts are full of milk,
and his bones are moistened with marrow.
Yet shall he be brought to the grave, and shall
remain in the tomb. The clods of the valley
shall be sweet unto him, and every man shall
draw after him, as there are innumerable
before him.
(Job 21: 23-24, 32-33 KJV)

Nevertheless, these are exceptions and not the norm, and God could be giving such persons a very long rope. We may never be able to explain this but one must NEVER LEAN ON THE EXCEPTIONS TO WALK IN WICKEDNESS. You might not be that exempted.

Also By Boniface Keelson

LEAFS OF INSPIRATION

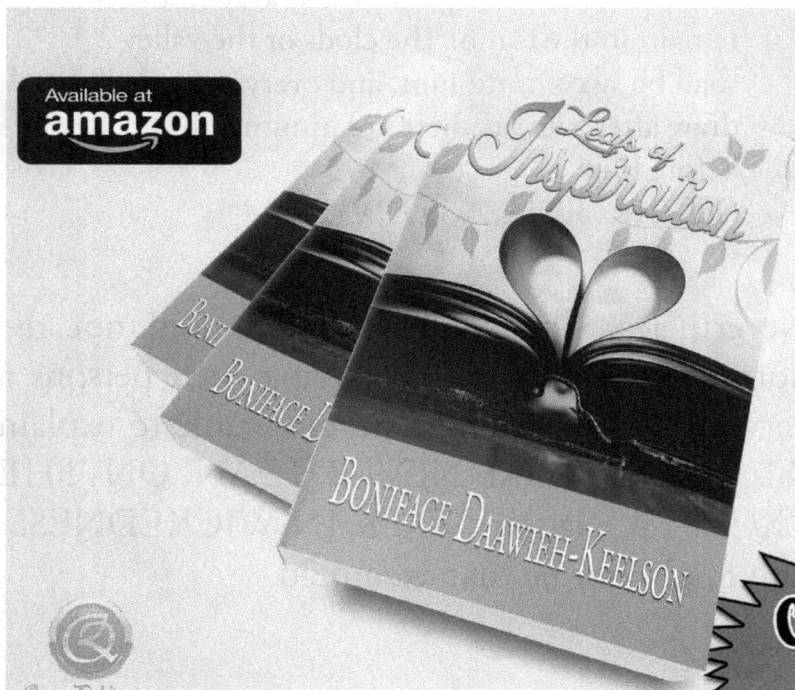

Everyone has a story...but until it is shared, it may never become a source of hope for those in despair to cling onto for survival.

Leafs of Inspiration is a collection of stories of hope—stories that will inspire you and strengthen your faith in the Lord. Discover fresh hope for your walk with God as Pastor Boniface bears his heart out and shares his experiences in life and ministry.

*9 7 8 1 9 8 8 4 3 9 0 4 4 *